JARROLD
leisure

Fort William

Compiled by
Hugh Taylor

JARROLD
publishing

Mapping
sourced from
Ordnance
Survey®

Text: Hugh Taylor
Photography: Hugh Taylor
Editor: Crawford Gillan
Designer: Sarah Crouch

© Jarrold Publishing 2004

 Ordnance Survey® This product includes mapping data licensed from Ordnance Survey® with the permission of the Controller of Her Majesty's Stationery Office. © Crown Copyright 2004. All rights reserved. Licence number 100017593. Ordnance Survey, the OS symbol and Pathfinder are registered trademarks and Explorer, Landranger and Outdoor Leisure are trademarks of the Ordnance Survey, the national mapping agency of Great Britain.

Jarrold Publishing
ISBN 0-7117-3006-7

First published 2004
by Jarrold Publishing

Printed in Belgium
by Proost NV, Turnhout. 1/04

Jarrold Publishing
Pathfinder Guides, Whitefriars,
Norwich NR3 1JR
E-mail: info@totalwalking.co.uk
www.totalwalking.co.uk

Front cover: Glencoe
Previous page: Loch Leven

Contents

Keymap

SCALE 1:384 615 or 1 INCH to about 6 MILES *1CM to 3.8KM*

0   2   4   6   8   10 KILOMETRES   15

0   2   4   6   MILES   8   10

KEYMAP HEIGHTS SHOWN IN FEET

Introduction

The walks in this book have been devised specifically with families and children in mind. All of the walks have points of interest and a question designed to keep young minds occupied.

Don't be surprised if the landscape looks familiar. If you think you've seen it before the chances are you have, at the movies. The hills, glens and castles on these walks appear as major stars or as supporting cast in films like *Highlander*, *Rob Roy*, *Braveheart* and *Local Hero*. Children will be attracted to the Harry Potter connection at Glenfinnan, where the Hogwarts Express crossed the massive viaduct with Ron and Harry in hot pursuit in a flying Ford Anglia. During the summer, you can take a ride on the steam train that starred as the Hogwarts Express. Farther south in Glencoe is where Hagrid's Hut stood during filming of the third Harry Potter movie.

The walks are mainly in the ancient lordship of Lochaber, which extended from Loch Leven in the south to Glen Garry in the north and from Badenoch in the east to Moidart in the west. We cross briefly into Appin, traditional home of the Stewarts of Appin for a few interesting walks and stories.

Mallaig harbour

Many of the walks on forest roads and footpaths are waymarked and are easy walking even in winter. If you have not done much walking then start with the shorter routes at the front of the book. Even there, you will find a few walks that have short but steep climbs. The trick is to slow down and take short steps. Walk at a pace that will allow you to carry on a conversation without too much effort.

An ancient footpath

One of the delights of walking in this part of Scotland is the history. Complete all of the walks and you will have had an introduction to some of the major events in Scotland's past. Massive geological upheavals shaped the landscape from the beginning of time to the end of the last ice age and from the legendary days of Ossian and Fionn MacCumhail to the rise and decline of industrialisation, people have left their marks on the land.

Follow Bonnie Prince Charlie from his landing at Moidart, where he raised his standard at Glenfinnan at the start of the Jacobite Rising in 1745 to his retreat through remnants of the ancient Caledonian pine forest. Cross lonely heather-clad hills to the cave, where he hid while on the run from Government troops after defeat at Culloden in 1746.

Walk along sections of the military roads built after Culloden and used to suppress and dismantle the highlanders' traditional way of life. Visit the scene of a bloody and deliberate act of genocide in Glencoe where the King personally signed the papers ordering the killing of unarmed men, women and children, simply to set an example to others. In Glen Duror, to the west of Glencoe, find out how dispossessed highlanders plotted a revenge that ended in murder. This then entered the pages of Robert Louis Stevenson's *Kidnapped*, where fact merged with fiction to provide the author with a 'ripping yarn'. In the novel James of the Glen is accused of the murder, tried by a rigged jury and executed. On a hilltop above the Ballachulish bridge you'll find a memorial on the spot where James was actually killed and where his body was put in chains and hung from the gibbet for months. The Appin Murder is still a controversial subject in these parts and has never been solved.

The building of the military roads in the second half of the 18th century changed this wild and remote place, opening it up to the same new ways that the agrarian revolution had brought elsewhere in the country. Clan chiefs, most now living remote from their people in London and Edinburgh, required an increased income from their estates to finance lavish new lifestyles. To this end, they cleared their tenants out to make way for more lucrative sheep. This black act now known as the Highland Clearances was carried out by force. People were evicted from their homes by armed men and the roofs set on fire to prevent their return. On a couple of the walks in this book you'll go through the remains of some of these townships. The Clearances and several years when the potato crop failed led to the exodus of thousands of people from the Highlands, many settling in Canada, America and Australia.

The Industrial Revolution also brought changes, albeit not as great as those of the agrarian reforms. Telford's Caledonian Canal, built to join three lochs along the geological fault known as the Great Glen, was one of the industrial marvels of its day. Production increased at the

Boats on Loch Leven, near Ballachullish

Glencoe

Ballachulish slate quarries. Farther down Loch Leven an abundance of water and high mountains provided an ideal situation for generating hydro-electricity at Kinlochleven. The electricity was used to run the aluminium smelter there and that tiny town was one of the first in Britain to have electric street lighting. Farther west at Strontian, lead mines were providing the raw materials to make musket balls for the British Army. It was here that a new mineral, strontianite was discovered, from which the element strontium was later isolated. As industry proliferated, this part of Scotland grew briefly prosperous, but a combination of diminishing raw materials, poor transport links, cheap foreign imports and multi-national companies led to each of these ventures shutting.

However, leisure and tourism are now drawing more people to this majestic mountain landscape with its hidden glens, waterfalls and lochs. You can walk by snow-capped peaks reflected in still lochs or head up a deep glen enclosed by massive glacial rocks. Enjoy the bright green of native birch and rowan in spring, the summer purple of heather-clad hills, the russet tones of turning leaves and bracken or the black winter crags, etching their shapes on a land of snow or blurred into swirling mist.

1 Glenfinnan Viaduct and the Hogwarts Express

Harry Potter meets Bonnie Prince Charlie and some of Scotland's most atmospheric scenery. This is the view the boy wizard and his pals see from the windows of the Hogwarts Express. It's also where Prince Charlie and his supporters landed. Looking down Loch Sheil on a hazy morning, it is easy to imagine a rowing boat slowly emerging from the mist.

START A830 at the Glenfinnan Visitor Centre
DISTANCE 2½ miles (4km)
TIME 1½ hours
PARKING National Trust Visitor Centre Glenfinnan (pay)
ROUTE FEATURES Lanes and pavements; woodland; rough and boggy hillside

Jacobites were supporters of the deposed Royal House of Stewart. They staged two rebellions. The first, in 1715, was over almost before it started. The second, in 1745, saw Bonnie Prince Charlie lead his forces south as far as Derby before retreating north to a final and total defeat at Culloden on April 16. The Prince escaped and spent five months on the run in the Highlands before escaping to France, but it was the end of the Jacobite dream.

The Glenfinnan monument

Cross the road from the visitor centre car park and turn right along the footpath. Cross a bridge then turn first left towards Slatach.

PUBLIC TRANSPORT Rail or bus service from Fort William
REFRESHMENTS There is a restaurant in the visitor centre
PICNIC TABLES At visitor centre car park
ORDNANCE SURVEY MAPS Explorer 398 (Loch Morar & Mallaig)

A Walk along this heavily-wooded country lane, past the entrance to the Glenfinnan House Hotel and when the road curves left opposite a wooden house, fork right onto a rough road heading uphill.

B This continues for some way. Keep going until the road rejoins the main road near the Princes House Hotel. Cross the road then turn right.

C Turn left and head uphill toward the railway station. When the first carriage appears on the right look for a sign to the right of it pointing to a 'woodland walk and viewpoint'. Continue behind the carriage and follow the path into the wood. This is a well-maintained and pleasant path with railway sleepers over the worst boggy bits. When the path forks follow the signs for 'Viewpoint'. After leaving the woods, the path heads uphill on some steep steps then under the railway and through a gate to access the open hillside. From here there is a short steep section, which is rough and boggy. Take your time and at the top of the hill it eases off. Follow the path as it runs parallel to the railway. Although boggy the going is fairly easy but there are a couple of bits where the path goes over rocky ground and *care should be*

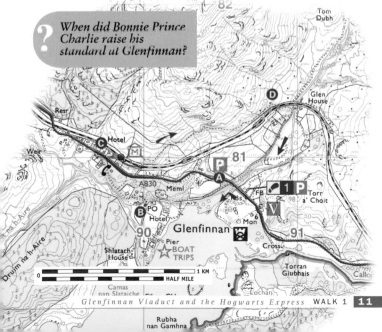

> **?** *When did Bonnie Prince Charlie raise his standard at Glenfinnan?*

Glenfinnan viaduct on Fort William to Mallaig line

taken. The view of the viaduct from the highest point of the walk makes all the effort worthwhile and it's the best spot to take a photograph. Check the timings of the Jacobite steam train and get to this point just before it's due at Glenfinnan. This was the train that doubled as the Hogwarts Express in the Harry Potter film. It was while it was crossing the Glenfinnan Viaduct that Harry and Ron caught up with it in a flying Ford Anglia.

D Head down towards the start of the viaduct and go through a gate in the deer fence, through the arch and follow the path until it reaches a metalled lane. Turn right and follow this back to the road. Turn left and return to the car park. ●

The **Road to the Isles** from Fort William to Mallaig follows the centuries old route used by the people of the islands. This area of dramatic scenery is called **Garbh Chriochan**, the rough bounds, in Gaelic. Modern transport links have opened up access to Morar and Moidart but venture across the water in the small ferry to the trackless wilderness of Knoydart and you will get some idea of how isolated and inaccessible this place was just over a century ago.

Neptune's Staircase and the Caledonian Canal

2

START Neptune's Staircase by the B8004 at Banavie

DISTANCE 2 miles (3.2km)

TIME 1½ hours

PARKING Public car park next to the Moorings Hotel (free)

ROUTE FEATURES Canal paths; a short, wet tunnel

A splendid but short stroll along the banks of Thomas Telford's masterpiece of civil engineering. Leaving the bustle and noise of the locks with their massive gates of pine-covered iron, enter a peaceful, waterway haven of easy walking, flanked by hawthorn and deciduous woodland, where the only sounds are birdsong and the occasional boat's engine.

Park at the back of the car park then look for a gate leading to the canal. Head downhill to the first lock and cross the canal.

A Turn left and walk up the steps by each of the eight locks. In the short space of 550 yds (500m) the level of the canal is raised by some 64 ft (20m). Look out for the houses on your left with the bow-fronted windows. These were originally lock-keepers' houses and the large windows allowed them a clear view along the canal so they could see when a vessel was approaching.

Pause for a moment when you reach the top and enjoy the view back downhill. Continue along the canal towpath on the Great Glen Way, a long-distance foot and cycle path. Go through a gate and continue alongside the canal.

The canal was built to let boats avoid the long and hazardous crossing of the Pentland Firth when sailing from the east to the west coast.

After about ½ mile (800m) look out for two metal gates close together on your right hand side.

PUBLIC TRANSPORT Rail or bus service from Fort William

REFRESHMENTS The Moorings Hotel does meals and snacks all day
Children's area and picnic tables available in car park

PUBLIC TOILETS Nearest are at Killmallie Hall in Corpach a mile away

ORDNANCE SURVEY MAPS Explorer 392 (Ben Nevis & Fort William)

Thomas Telford, the engineer responsible for the Caledonian Canal, was one of the most versatile and prolific engineers of the Industrial Revolution. The son of a Dumfriesshire shepherd, he worked initially as a stone mason in the Scottish Borders before progressing to work on projects as diverse as churches, roads, bridges and canals. He was the first President of the Institute of Civil Engineers and is best remembered for his work on the Caledonian Canal and the Menai Suspension Bridge.

B Go through the first one and head downhill, on a grassy lane, back towards the locks. When the lane reaches a burn, ford this then turn right beside some telegraph poles to reach a double tunnel under the canal. Go through the left-hand tunnel. This can be wet in places making wellingtons or good boots an essential item of kit. Exit the tunnel, turn sharp left and head up the canal banking to regain the path. Follow this path back towards Banavie. You will encounter a locked gate, which you can climb over or bypass. From here the path continues back to the locks. Head downhill, passing the Moorings Hotel to return to the car park.

> **?** *What is the name of the largest mountain you can see looking south-east from the locks?*

Neptune's Staircase

At the end of the Caledonian Canal, a mile away (1.6km) is the town of Corpach. Roughly translated this means the Place of the Bodies. It was here that the remains of the great and the good were brought to be put on board a ship bound for burial on the holy island of Iona.

Mist-shrouded mountains

The **Caledonian Canal**, opened in 1822, is one of the greatest British engineering achievements of the 19th century. This is Scotland's longest canal, stretching for 60 miles (97km), with the lengths of Lochs Lochy, Oich and Ness providing about 40 miles (64km) of it. The remaining 20 miles had to be dug out by hand. Of the 29 locks, the series of eight, known as Neptune's Staircase, is the finest engineering feat of the whole canal.

3 *Crofters Wood*

START A861 just north of the ferry jetty at Camusnagaul

DISTANCE 1¾ miles (2.8km)

TIME 1 hour

PARKING In Fort William then take the ferry across the loch. Limited parking at the start of the walk

ROUTE FEATURES Woodland; hill; shores of Loch Linnhe

This short walk passes through a mature community woodland, teeming with animal and plant life, then continues along a coastline frequented by graceful heron and playful otters. A couple of viewpoints amply repay the effort needed to reach them by providing unrivalled views over Loch Linnhe to Fort William and beyond to Ben Nevis.

🖉 From the ferry landing turn right, go along the road a short distance to a cattle-grid. Cross this and immediately on the left side of the road is the first red waymark.

Ⓐ Head uphill on a short, steep climb through the woods. This is a well waymarked path and it is impossible to go wrong.

Ⓑ Go through a kissing-gate and turn right onto a path running beside the ruins of a wall. Follow this well-trodden path through the woods and then onto open hillside. When you reach a deer fence turn left and follow the line of it uphill. A waymarker points left indicating

Fungi en route

a viewpoint with a seat. From here on a clear day you can enjoy a grand view over Loch Linnhe to Fort William with Ben Nevis in the

PUBLIC TRANSPORT Ferry from Fort William

PUBLIC TOILETS None

REFRESHMENTS Fort William or the Corran Inn

ORDNANCE SURVEY MAPS Explorer 392 (Ben Nevis & Fort William)

Many **wild orchids** are found in Scotland but in the northwest the most prolific is the heath spotted variety. It's one of the few orchids that tolerates acid soil, which is why it is found in the bogs and moors of this region. The colours of the petals vary from pale pink to purple. Even the spotted markings show considerable variation and it is possible to think that two similar plants are different species.

background. Return to the path then head towards the mast on the hill above you. It's a bit of a pull up to the top but worth it for the view. Retrace your steps to the path and follow it to the next waymarker.

When did the local community centre stop being used as a school?

ⓒ Turn right, go through a kissing-gate and head downhill on another well waymarked trail.

In the autumn this part of the wood has abundant displays of fungi from the bright red fly agaric to the orange yellow false chanterelle.

The **yellow flag iris** grows well in waterlogged ground and can be found in the many boggy parts of this walk. They grow from an underground stem called a rhizome. During the spring long green leaves like blades grow up to a metre in length. By June and July the bright yellow flowers produce a burst of colour with each plant producing up to a dozen blooms.

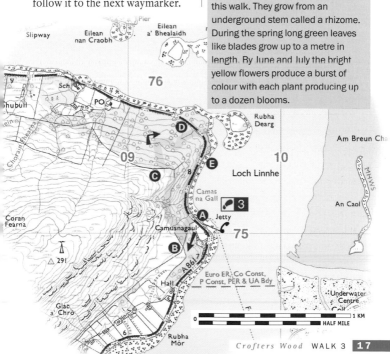

Loch Linnhe

D At the bottom of the hill cross a burn, then the road and into the woods along the shoreline. Follow the path through the woods or go onto the beach and follow the shoreline.

While walking along the shores of Loch Linnhe keep an eye out for grey herons. These have a distinctive yellow beak and legs and a long neck. They are most likely to be spotted standing motionless by the edge of the water stalking an unsuspecting fish. They make nests of sticks in the high tree tops, returning each year to the same nesting site. Their mating rituals are elaborate and very noisy. Eggs hatch about four weeks after they are laid and the young chicks are out of the nest by the time they are eight weeks old.

Along the shore you will come across a bench fastened to the top of some rocks in an ideal picnic spot. If you are very quiet you may spot the shy and elusive otter. Although they are usually nocturnal they are sometimes seen during the day hunting for food. They live on a diet of fish, eels and crabs, which they hunt among the seaweed. They also eat small mammals, insects and even slugs.

Return to the path through the woods and follow it till it joins the main road.

E Turn left and return to the ferry.

Bonnie Prince Charlie's Cave and Chia-Aig Waterfall

4

START Car park at the Waterfall
DISTANCE 2½ miles (4km)
TIME 1½ hours
PARKING On the B8005 north from Gairlochy and 1½ miles (2.4km) beyond Clunes (free)
ROUTE FEATURES Well-surfaced woodland paths and forest roads. Rather a steep climb initially

Set against a backdrop of lochs and mountains, history and nature combine at Chia-Aig to produce one of the most fascinating and attractive walks in Lochaber. This remnant of the ancient Caledonian pine forest contains trees, which were old when Bonnie Prince Charlie used them for shelter more than two and a half centuries ago.

The native woodlands on this walk provide homes for a variety of wildlife including some **rare species**. Look out for the red squirrels scurrying through the trees or climbing up trunks. You may be fortunate to catch a glimpse of a wryneck or a crested tit. As non-native trees are removed, allowing the Scots pine forest to regenerate, more rare species like the capercaillie may return.

Walk from the car park along to the falls. According to local folklore the large pool they cascade into is known as the Witches Cauldron and has the power to diminish their spells. Turn right and head uphill on a steep, well-paved path. At a junction with a larger path turn left and follow the sign for Prince Charlie's Cave Walk.

? *What emblem did the warriors of Clan Cameron wear on their clothing in battle?*

PUBLIC TRANSPORT None
PUBLIC TOILETS None on route
REFRESHMENTS Banavie or Fort William
PICNIC AREA At the Falls
ORDNANCE SURVEY MAP Explorer 400 (Loch Lochy & Glen Roy)

Head steadily uphill through the woods to reach another T-junction.

A Turn right following the Forest Walks arrow. The path continues to rise through the forest then reaches open hillside. If you are finding the going a bit tough just slow down a bit and get your breath back. The paths are excellent and you will have no trouble if you take it easy. Remember Bonnie Prince Charlie never had it this good.

Eventually, you will reach the summit of the hill by a lone Scots pine and an interpretation board. Pause for a moment here to enjoy the majestic view along Loch Arkaig.

From this point continue in the same direction now heading downhill to meet a forest road.

B Turn left and at the next junction turn right at a signpost pointing to Prince Charlie's Cave. After a further 200 yds (183km) a sign indicates a left turn.

C Go up a steep path here and follow it to its conclusion at the cave. In reality this is just a small natural shelter formed from two large boulders. Squeeze inside and try it for size and comfort. It will give you some idea of the discomfort the Prince endured living rough, while Government redcoats hunted him after his flight from Culloden.

Bonnie Prince Charlie's Cave

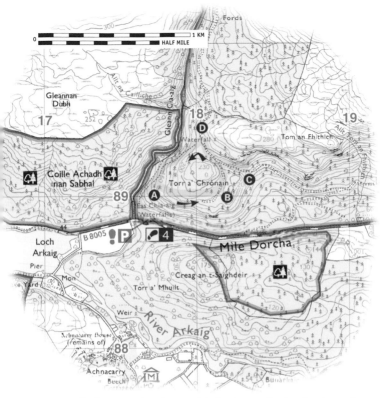

Return to the forest road and turn right. After 200 yds (183km) turn right again at a forest walk sign.

D Another few hundred yards (274km) along this road look out for another forest walk sign and turn left to go down some stairs into dense woodland. Head downhill keeping right at the first junction to return to the top of the falls. Keep left here and follow the path back to the car park. Finally take the path from here up to the belvedere and enjoy the views of the pinewoods of Loch Arkaig. ●

> On the far side of **Loch Arkaig** several tall dead trees can be seen in the remnants of the pine forest. They died as a result of fires started by **commandos**, who trained here during the Second World War. Because it has thick bark the Scots pine is relatively fire resistant, which is why only a few were destroyed. Charring is still evident on several trunks.

5 Glen Loy and Errachat Oakwoods

START Just off the B8004 north of Banavie

DISTANCE 2½miles (4km)

TIME 1½ hours

PARKING Car park at beginning of walk (free)

ROUTE FEATURES Forest roads; a woodland path

The forest at Glen Loy was planted with spruce in the early days of the Forestry Commission way back in the 1930s. Most of this has now been harvested and during replanting the area of native woodland has been increased. Semi-natural oak and other broadleaved seedlings can be seen round the existing area of ancient woodland.

Go through a gate at the end of the car park and head along the forest road for just short of half a mile (800m).

The roads here are very quiet and there's every chance that you may spot some of the wildlife that lives here. In particular, look out for some magnificent buzzards. You may see them soaring high above the woods, hanging, almost motionless, in the wind as they stalk a small mammal or perched on top of a dead tree trunk.

Nesting box, Erracht Oakwoods

PUBLIC TRANSPORT None

PUBLIC TOILETS None on route

REFRESHMENTS The Moorings Hotel, Banavie

ORDNANCE SURVEY MAPS Explorer 392 (Ben Nevis & Fort William)

The oakwoods here are home to a wide range of plants and animals. Depending on which season you visit you could find colourful displays of **bluebells** and **primroses**, all manner of ferns mosses and lichens and a host of fungi.

A At a fork in the road go left following the forest walk sign.

B At the next fork go right. As you continue along this road you will see many examples of native trees that have re-seeded naturally. When you reach some large oak trees on the right side of the path, stop. Opposite them is a forest walk sign.

C Turn left here and follow the footpath downhill through Erracht woodland.

At the start of the 20th century the area covered by woodland in Britain had declined to five per cent. This was due to long-term over-use of timber in building, charcoal creation and for fuel. The creation of the Forestry Commission was a measure aimed at reversing the decline and the early years of the century saw much planting of mainly foreign conifers. The area now covered by woodland has risen to 12 per cent.

What can you see attached to the trunks of some of the trees?

Changing trends and the emphasis on native species has seen the commission re-plant vast areas with native species and the forests are now managed on a sustainable basis with the emphasis on using woodland as an economic, environmental and social resource.

> Did you know that **oak trees** grow for 200 years then live for another 200 before spending up to a further 200 slowly dying?

D At the junction with a forest road turn left again. Follow this road, which runs beside the River Loy for a time before swinging away to the left. Look out for the distinctive, sticky black droppings of the pine-marten. This shy creature lives in the trees and is like a large ferret. Occasionally you may catch a fleeting glimpse of one. When you reach the first road junction keep right and again at the second. Return from here to the car park. ●

Forest road through the Oakwoods

Steil Falls and the Nevis Gorge

START Car park at the end of Glen Nevis NN167690

DISTANCE 2½miles (4km)

TIME 1½ hours

PARKING At the end of the Glen Nevis Road (free)

ROUTE FEATURES Rocky path, narrow and steep in places

6

Described by mountaineer W H Murray as 'Himalayan in character', the Nevis Gorge is like a fragment of some exotic far distant land, tucked secretly into the Scottish landscape. Rocky crags rise above wooded slopes, while white water rushes downhill in a torrent. Dappled sunlight filters through the leaves of the oak, Scots pine, birch and rowan trees that surround the path.

Leave the car park and head along the gorge on a well-surfaced footpath.

Almost immediately you will come across a sign warning that the path becomes increasingly dangerous towards the gorge and that fatal accidents have occurred. It advises walkers to 'proceed with great care'. Someone with a sense of humour has placed the skull and horns of a dead sheep on top of the sign. Bear in mind that most accidents are caused by people wearing inappropriate footwear. *Wear sturdy walking boots or shoes and walk carefully and you will have no problems on this well-used and popular family walk.*

Looking up Nevis Gorge

PUBLIC TRANSPORT None

PUBLIC TOILETS None on route

REFRESHMENTS Fort William or the Café Beag just past the youth hostel

PICNIC TABLES By the riverside just past the lower car park

ORDNANCE SURVEY MAPS Explorer 392 (Ben Nevis & Fort William)

? *Which remote railway station can be reached on foot from this path?*

Proceed along the path, which follows the line of the gorge.

Take care when you reach a slippy, rocky section that crosses a burn. Just around the corner from this, the path forks. Keep left and follow the path along the contours of the gorge.

The gorge and surrounding mountains are created from several different types of rock. Mostly Dalradian schist but with granite intrusions from the Devonian times. The lower slopes of Ben Nevis are formed from this granite. On Sgurr a' Mhaim, the second highest summit of the Mamores, you can see the pale grey scree of Dalradian quartzite. Examine the rock as you walk along to try to find examples of igneous intrusions created eons ago when hot magma was forced up through a fault in the schist to create dykes.

The water of Nevis

Cross a larger burn by a wooden bridge. From here on there are several rocky parts of the path to negotiate and *this is where you need to exercise care*. Head up some steps in the rock and along a boardwalk. The path is steeper from this point with several natural stone steps to climb. Eventually the gorge opens out into a flat valley and you'll get your first look at the falls in the distance.

The path splits at this point.

A Keep to the obviously made-up path to avoid erosion and keep going till you reach the river. This is the best view of the falls. *To go any farther involves crossing a hairy, scary, chain bridge, which can be dangerous and is not recommended.*

Return by the same route. ●

> Steall Falls is the third highest, but possibly the most impressive waterfall in Scotland. Translated from the Gaelic, its name means **white spout**. It is at its best after heavy rain or in the depths of winter when it freezes over and you can watch climbers going up it like flies using two ice axes and crampons to get a grip.

7 Signal Rock and the Massacre of Glencoe

START From the car park on the site of the former visitor centre

DISTANCE 2 miles (3.2km)

TIME 1 hour

PARKING Just off the A82 at the former visitor centre site (free)

ROUTE FEATURES Forest paths; a narrow lane; rough ground

The cold-blooded murder in the early morning of February 14, 1692, of the MacDonalds of Glencoe by men of Clan Campbell serving as Government soldiers was a terrible abuse of the ancient Highland obligation of hospitality. This short woodland walk goes to the spot traditionally believed to be where the signal to kill was given.

Walk towards the river and cross the bridge. Go through a gate and turn immediately left then follow the path to a junction.

A Go left following the signs for Signal Rock.

In an attempt to quell Jacobite unrest the Government insisted that clan chiefs sign an oath of loyalty by January 1, 1692. MacIain of Glencoe procrastinated then went in error to Inverlochy only to be told he had gone to the wrong place. Battling against dreadful weather, MacIain finally made it to Inveraray and, although a few days late, his oath was accepted.

But the Government took the decision to use this to make an example of the Glencoe MacDonalds. The Secretary of State for Scotland, John Dalrymple of Stair, initiated the orders for the 'Massacre' but they were signed by the King. They made it clear that no mercy should be shown.

PUBLIC TRANSPORT Bus service from Fort William

PUBLIC TOILETS Nearest at Glencoe Visitor Centre a little farther along the A82 or in Glencoe village

REFRESHMENTS At the Clachaig Inn provided your name is not Campbell

ORDNANCE SURVEY MAPS Explorer 384 (Glen Coe & Glen Etive)

On February 1 the Earl of Argyll's regiment was dispatched to Glencoe and billeted on the inhabitants. The unwritten rules of Highland hospitality demanded the MacDonalds provide food and shelter to anyone who asked for it, even their enemies, the Campbells.

At a clearing the path forks by a large tree. Keep left. Go through a gate, following the path to a crossroads by a wooden barrier.

B Cross here and head uphill through the woods on steps eventually to reach the rock.

Tradition in Glencoe has it that a fire was lit on Signal Rock as a sign to the troops that the killing was to begin. Commanding the troops was Captain Robert Campbell of Glenlyon. His orders were absolutely clear: 'You are hereby ordered to fall upon the rebels, the MacDonalds of Glencoe, and put all to the sword under 70.'

Glencoe can be a dark and foreboding place, almost like a landscape from Tolkien's **Lord of the Rings**. From its entrance, guarded by Buchaille Etive Mor rising out of Rannoch Moor, it runs for 10 miles (16km), to meet Loch Leven. Shut in on both sides for most of its length by the wild and rugged mountains that have attracted several generations of mountaineers, it eventually opens out into a softer landscape towards its end.

At the signal the soldiers fell upon their unsuspecting hosts indiscriminately killing men, women and children as they slept or as they tried to escape from their beds. MacIain, his wife and his two sons perished, as did 34 other members of his clan. A further two companies of soldiers had been ordered to march over the hills from Kinlochleven to block the glen at first light but they failed to appear, allowing some MacDonalds to escape. Many of them subsequently died of exposure in the snow-filled passes.

Return by the same route but turn left **A** onto the path signposted for An Tor. Follow this to reach signs for the Clachaig Inn. Go over a stile and then through a kissing-gate and turn right onto the road.

> **?** Who gave Signal Rock and the small strip of land round it to the National Trust for Scotland in 1936?

Pass the Clachaig then turn right **C** onto a path and follow it to the bank of the river then turn left over the bridge to return to the car park.

The 'Massacre' backfired on the Government and presented a wonderful propaganda opportunity to the Jacobites. Although the Campbells were traditional enemies of the MacDonalds they were enlisted Government soldiers and just following orders. To this day, however, there is still a sign in the Clachaig Inn proclaiming 'No Hawkers or Campbells'. ●

Dark and foreboding Glencoe

Glencoe Lochan

8

START	Lochan car park in Glencoe village
DISTANCE	2 miles (3.2km)
TIME	1 hour
PARKING	Lochan car park (free)
ROUTE FEATURES	Well-surfaced footpaths with some climbing

This is a combination of three, waymarked Forestry Commission walks. The mountain walk at the start is steep but worth the climb for the views at the top. The woodland walk is an easy stroll through delightful woods with grand views along Loch Leven at a couple of viewpoints and the lochan walk is wheelchair friendly.

Leave the car park following the blue waymarked route and go up some steps. The path climbs steeply through woodland to reach the top of the hill where a well-placed picnic table offers the chance of a rest and a grand view along the ridges of Beinn a' Bheithir as well as along Loch Leven and past the Ballachulish Bridge to Loch Linnhe and beyond to the outline of Garbh Bheinn.

Just past here the path leads off to the right and uphill for a short distance to another viewpoint with a bench.

Glencoe village is tiny and really has only one street. This was the end of the old road through the glen. The village attracts a large number of walkers and climbers all the year round. The only attraction, apart from its stunning natural location, is the old thatched cottage that houses the **folk museum**.

The woodland has a variety of conifers and deciduous trees including some good examples of Douglas fir and Sequoia.

A Continue on the path along the top of the hill then start down the other side towards the lochan.

PUBLIC TRANSPORT Bus from Fort William
REFRESHMENTS One of the best places in this area is the tourist information centre at nearby Ballachulish
PICNIC TABLES Found at various points of the walk
PUBLIC TOILETS In the car park in Glencoe village
ORDNANCE SURVEY MAPS Explorer 384 (Glen Coe & Glen Etive)

B At a T-junction turn right where you will find another strategically placed picnic table. Head anti-clockwise round the lochan path. A number of floating platforms can be accessed from the path. They are intended for fishing but provide good viewpoints for looking back across the lochan and up to the Pap of Glencoe.

The lochan was built by Lord Strathcona, when he acquired the estate in the late 19th century. He also built Glencoe House and laid out the woodlands. David Alexander Smith was born in Forres in 1820, the son of a shepherd. At the age of 18 he emigrated to Canada, where he became the first Governor of the Hudson's Bay Company, High Commissioner for Canada and later was created Lord Strathcona. The estate woods were bought by the Forestry Commission in 1950.

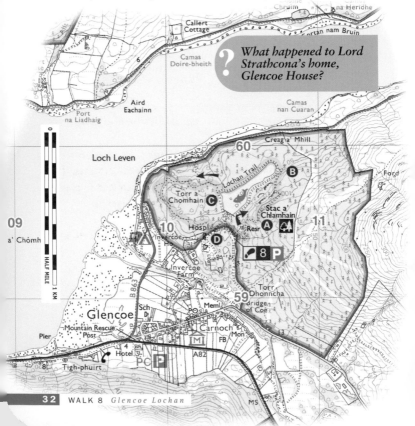

? *What happened to Lord Strathcona's home, Glencoe House?*

Glencoe Lochan

You may have noticed **Indian feathers** depicted on the signs and marker posts. Lord Strathcona married a Canadian, whose grandmother was a native American. She had been born and brought up near Hudson Bay so he created Glencoe Estate to resemble her homeland in an attempt to alleviate her homesickness. It didn't work and his wife never settled.

C At the next junction turn right onto the footpath for the yellow walk. Follow the markers to another spot with a picnic table and this time with a view across the loch to Ballachullish.

Continue on this path and when it forks, keep left.

D At the next junction turn right, then immediately left, go down some steps and turn left onto a path. This takes you past a small pond. From here go through a gate at the end of the path to return to the car park ●

9 *Ardgour*

Ardgour is a mountainous part of Lochaber bounded to the north by Loch Eil, Loch Linnhe to the east, Loch Sheil to the west and in the south by Loch Sunart and Glen Tarbert. But there are no mountains on this pleasant, flat walk through two pretty townships which form the gateway to Ardnamurchan and Mull.

START The Inn at Ardgour
DISTANCE 3¼ miles (5km)
TIME 2 hours
PARKING At Corran Ferry (free) or Corran beside the jetty (free)
ROUTE FEATURES Minor roads; country lanes; forest tracks; beach

The building opposite the ferry slipway is The Inn at Ardgour. Originally this was a ferryman's cottage built to replace one razed in 1746, when, in the aftermath of Culloden, the Duke of Cumberland used terror tactics to subdue the Highlanders. As part of this strategy a detachment of troops from Fort William swept through the area laying waste to homes and murdering the inhabitants.

Walk north from The Inn along the road to North Corran and visit Ardgour church.

This was built by Thomas Telford,

? When was Ardgour church built and how much did it cost?

the great civil engineer, who built the Caledonian Canal. This is one of many churches designed by Telford in the Highlands as part of a Parliamentary project for the Church of Scotland. The site was gifted to the community by the 13th Laird of Ardgour, Colonel Alexander Maclean.

The bay opposite the church is called An Camus Aiseag, the bay of the ferry, and the original jetty was nearby.

PUBLIC TRANSPORT Bus from Fort William to Corran Ferry then a short ferry crossing (free for pedestrians)
PUBLIC TOILETS Back of The Inn at Ardgour
REFRESHMENTS The Inn at Ardgour serves food all day
ORDNANCE SURVEY MAPS Explorer 391 (Ardgour & Strontian)

A Pass the church and take the first turning on the left, passing a house and entering an estate road via a gate. This is the east drive to Ardgour House and part of Ardgour Estate. The road is lined with deciduous trees, conifers and rhododendrons. Ignore the turning to the left. This runs between the two lochans and is the drive to Ardvulin House. The lochans, or 'kettle holes' were formed during the last ice age. Large boulders from receding glaciers made the holes, which became the lochans. The two you pass are called Lochan nah Eaglais, the loch of the church, and Lochan Eoin Mhic Alistair, the Loch of Ian son of Alistair, and in all probability one of the Maclean lairds.

When the road forks keep left, cross a bridge then, at the junction with a metalled lane, turn left.

B Follow this until you go through a gate to reach the road, which runs through the crofting community of Clovullin. *The general store is opposite this if you feel in need of a snack.*

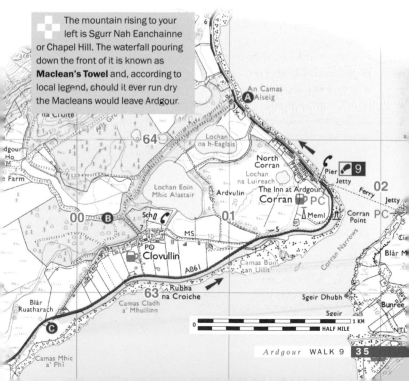

The mountain rising to your left is Sgurr Nah Eanchainne or Chapel Hill. The waterfall pouring down the front of it is known as **Maclean's Towel** and, according to local legend, should it ever run dry the Macleans would leave Ardgour.

Clovullin means the burial place by the mill but neither mill nor cemetery still exist. The building just beyond the village store is the Ardgour Memorial Hall, dedicated to the memory of the 16th Laird, Alexander John Maclean, who died in 1930, and his wife Muriel. When the hall was renovated in 1989 a plaque was erected to the memory of the 17th laird, Alexander's daughter Catriona.

Turn right onto the road and follow it to its junction with the main road, cross over, go down onto the beach and turn left.

If you are lucky you may spot the head of a grey seal bobbing up and down in the water. Towards the end of the day sea otters can also be seen and occasionally a heron may be spotted near the ferry jetty.

C Follow the shoreline along to the Corran Lighthouse. This is now an automated light but was once tended by two keepers, who lived on the premises. Its red light flashed to warn mariners approaching the Caledonian canal of the Corran Narrows.

From the lighthouse you can regain the road and return to the ferry. ●

The **Corran Narrows** is part of one of the oldest trade routes in the area. Before the days of the first ferry, drovers swum their cattle across Loch Linnhe on their way from the Inner Hebrides to sell them at Falkirk Tryst. The drovers crossed by hanging onto the long hair on the back of the cattle. When the first ferry, a rowing boat, was introduced their lives improved immensely.

The Inn at Ardgour

Inchree Waterfalls and General Wade's Road

The steep climb at the start of this walk is well repaid by the sight of the mighty waterfalls rushing down the hillside. A little farther on another steep climb is rewarded by the chance to walk along a piece of history, one of the first roads in the Highlands of Scotland.

START From the hamlet of Inchree, just south of the Corran Ferry on the A82 from Fort William
DISTANCE 3½ miles (5.6km)
TIME 2 hours
PARKING Forestry Commission Car Park (free)
ROUTE FEATURES Well-surfaced forest path, forest roads and old military road. Steep in parts

From the car park walk away from the interpretation board and follow the signs for the waterfall walk. Cross a small bridge and head uphill on a well-made path.

It's a fairly steep climb up to the falls but there are several strategically placed benches to ease the strain.

The Abhainn Righ cascades downhill from Gleann Righ over eight waterfalls, dropping about 150 ft (46km) to arrive at Inchree.

Also known as the Glen Righ Falls, they are at their best after a period of heavy rain. The path up to the falls traces the edge of a narrow gorge lined with birch, oak, ash and aspen. Look out for the short paths leading off the main route to fenced viewpoints where you can get the best views of the falls. Looking down to the river you may spot the odd grey wagtail or even a dipper flitting back and forth over the surface looking for lunch. Three of the falls are visible from this walk.

PUBLIC TRANSPORT Bus from Fort William
PUBLIC TOILETS At Corran Ferry
REFRESHMENTS Hotel at Corran Ferry
PICNIC TABLES In the car park.
ORDNANCE SURVEY MAPS Explorer 384 (Glen Coe & Glen Etive)

Continue past the falls and follow the path to the top of the hill where it ends in a T-junction with a forest road at a signpost for 'Wades Road Walk'.

General George Wade was dispatched to the Highlands to quell continued unrest after the failed Jacobite rising of 1715. Discovering that it was impossible to move troops and supplies without great difficulty, he proposed an intensive road building programme. As Military Commander in Scotland from 1726 to 1737, he was responsible for creating more than 250 miles (402km) of roads. Ironically Bonnie Prince Charlie used Wade's roads to move his army rapidly over long distances during the 1745 rebellion.

A Turn left and head along the road where you will have some clear views over Loch Linnhe to the hills of Kingairloch, Appin and Mull beyond.

B Look out for the spot where a footpath intersects the forest road and turn right following red waymarker posts uphill through dense woodland. This is quite a steep climb through spruce and larch and can be a bit on the dark side on a wet or overcast day. Several wooden bridges carry the footpath across various burns to reach a section of the old military road.

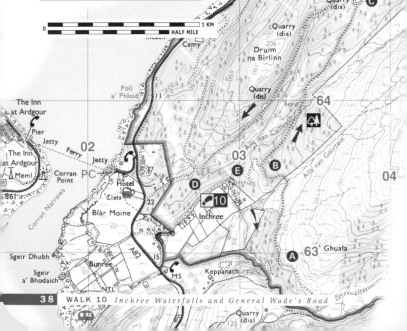

The hills of Ardgour

This dates back to the mid-18th century and was the original road to Fort William. Built after the battle of Culloden in 1746, it was intended to allow speedy movement of troops and supplies to and from the garrison at Fort William. This was all part of a deliberate strategy to dismantle the clan system and subdue the Highlands after the failed Jacobite Rising. Although called Wade's road, it was not built by the famous general but by his deputy and successor, General Caulfield.

C When the road reaches a crossroads beside an old, disused quarry, turn left onto a forest road. *The military road continues ahead from here over the hill to Corrychurachan and you can continue to follow it for a while before returning to this point to resume the walk.*

The forest road heads downhill for a considerable distance.

D When it bends right beside a bench look out for a 'Forest Walk' signpost and turn left into the forest. From here a steep, narrow path leads downhill through the woods.

E At the bottom of the hill leave the woods, cross a wooden bridge then turn left into the hamlet of Inchree and onto a forest road. Turn right and follow the red waymarkers back to the car park. ●

? *Where does the water that plunges over the falls end up?*

11 *Glen Duror*

START B3222 east of
Warren House Inn
DISTANCE 4 miles (6.4km)
TIME 1¾ hour
PARKING Start of walk
(free)
ROUTE FEATURES Forest
roads; woodland paths

*This forest walk is deep in the heart of
Appin, the setting for the Murder of the
Red Fox, an incident fictionalised in
Robert Louis Stevenson's* Kidnapped.
*David Balfour may have been a creation
of Stevenson's imagination but Alan
Breck Stewart and James of the Glen were
real people and the murder did take place.*

**? When was James of the
Glen hanged?**

Two signposts point the way
from the car park. One is for the
Duror Walk and the other to the
birthplace of James of the Glen.
Follow the forest road in the
direction indicated by the signs,
following the course of the
River Duror.

James of the Glen (Sheumais a'
Ghlinne) was James Stewart,
brother of Charles Stewart owner
of Ardsheal Estate in Appin. The
Stewarts had supported Bonnie
Prince Charlie during the Jacobite

Rising of 1745 and after his defeat
at Culloden, Charles Stewart fled
to France.

More than 90 Appin men died on
the battlefield at Culloden and in
the aftermath, Government troops
blitzed the area, confiscating
cattle and burning houses. The
estates of Jacobite supporters
were forfeited to the Crown,
Ardsheal being one of them.
The Government appointed
Colin Campbell of Glenure as
a factor to administer this and
three other estates. Before this
appointment James Stewart had
run the estate on behalf of his
absent brother.

PUBLIC TRANSPORT None
PUBLIC TOILETS None
REFRESHMENTS MacDonald Arms Hotel, Duror
ORDNANCE SURVEY MAPS Explorer 384 (Glen Coe & Glen Etive)

Keep going along the forest road following the waymarkers and ignoring two roads leading off from the left.

A When a waymarker points to the right leave the road and head downhill on a woodland path to cross a bridge over the river. Continue following this path as it climbs uphill and then comes down the other side.

Fly agaric en route

Although factor of the estate, Colin Campbell had problems collecting the rents. Most of the tenants preferred to keep paying it to their exiled chief. Glenure moved James Stewart from his home at Auchindarroch and rented it to a Campbell relative.

When Glenure received Government orders not to let land to Jacobites he served a series of eviction notices on several Ardsheil tenants. James, representing the tenants, took legal action to halt the evictions but others in the area, resentful of their lands being given to the hated Campbells, argued for a more direct action.

B Emerge from the woods into a surfaced turning area then

On May 14, 1752, **Colin Campbell of Glenure**, his nephew and a party of men were heading through the woods to the south of Ballachulish. A shot rang out and Glenure was hit. His nephew later described seeing a man with a gun running uphill away from the scene of the crime. Glenure was still conscious but later died from his wounds. One of the prime suspects was Alan Breck Stewart, a foster son of James of the Glen.

continue downhill on another forest road. After about another mile (1.6km), cross a gate and reach a junction.

C A signpost here points the way to Ach-charn and the home of James of the Glen. To get there, continue along this road to the farm of Ach-charn. The remains of James's dwelling is just beyond this.

Sign to Ach-charn

Wooded footpath through Glen Duror

Alan Breck Stewart fled to France after the murder of Glenure. He had gone there after Culloden and was serving in the French army. However he returned frequently to Appin to collect rents on behalf of his chief. A scapegoat was needed and James fitted the bill. He was hanged above the Ballachulish Ferry, where his body hung in chains for many years. Cairns mark the site of the murder and the gallows.

James moved to the smaller farmhouse of Ach-charn after his eviction from Auchindarroch. Despite this move, James remained on friendly terms with Glenure.

When Glenure was assassinated the day before the evictions were to take place a number of local people were suspected. The Government was concerned that the murder of their factor was a sign of further rebellion by the Jacobites and wanted an example made. James was arrested and tried in Inverary, the heart of Campbell country. The Duke of Argyll, chief of Clan Campbell, presided over the court and the jury was packed with Campbells. Although innocent of the crime, James was found guilty and sentenced to death. The Appin murder has never been solved. There are still Stewarts in Appin who know the identity of the murderer but they will never reveal it.

Return to the junction and continue along the forest road.

D When it ends at a T-junction turn right and follow this road uphill and back to the car park. ●

12

South Laggan and the Caledonian Canal

START	The locks just off the A82
DISTANCE	4 miles (6.4km)
TIME	2 hours
PARKING	Laggan Locks (free)
ROUTE FEATURES	Country lane; canal footpath; short main road section

Travelling along part of one of the world's most famous geological faults and the line of Thomas Telford's great marvel of the Industrial Age, this relatively flat and easy walk passes areas of unsurpassed scenic beauty. By way of contrast, it visits the site of one of Scotland's bloodiest battles and passes close to a well associated with an even more gruesome multiple beheading.

Turn left out of the car park and walk towards the canal and its two locks. A plaque passed on the way indicates the site of the Battle of the Shirts. This, in a part of Scotland famed for its clan feuds, was one of the bloodiest battles ever fought. In 1544, 300 men of Clan Fraser faced a combined force of MacDonalds and Camerons totalling 600. It was a hot day and fighting in the heavy woollen plaids that was the forerunner of the modern kilt proved impossible. So they cast them aside and attacked wearing nothing but their shirts. At the end of the battle only four Frasers and eight of their opponents were left alive.

Cross the bridge over the canal and go down a path between two cottages.

A Turn left at a waymarker and continue along a narrow tarmac lane. This passes some holiday chalets then crosses a cattle-grid before ending at a junction by a road.

PUBLIC TRANSPORT Bus service from Fort William
PUBLIC TOILETS None on walk
REFRESHMENTS The Inn on the Water when it is open, otherwise head for Invergarry
PICNIC TABLES Available at the car park
ORDNANCE SURVEY MAPS Explorer 400 (Loch Lochy & Glen Roy)

B Turn right and head uphill and along the road.

Keep on this road for just short of two miles (3.2km) to its junction with the A82 then turn right. Cross the A82 and walk along a rough path beside the road to reach Laggan Swing Bridge. This bridge spans the canal at the point where it enters Loch Oich.

Loch Oich is the shortest of the three lochs in the Great Glen at a little over four miles (6.4km). The railway from Spean Bridge to Fort Augustus used to run beside its southern shore but this is long gone. The track-bed now forms part of the Great Glen Way.

What is the other name of The Inn on the Water?

The **Great Glen** which runs from Inverness to Fort William is a famous geological fault created millions of years ago when the land on the north side of the glen slid 60 miles (97km) to the south. This split the Highlands into two parts, the Grampian Highlands, in the south and the Northern Highlands. The fault continues along Loch Linnhe and across the edge of the island of Mull towards Ireland.

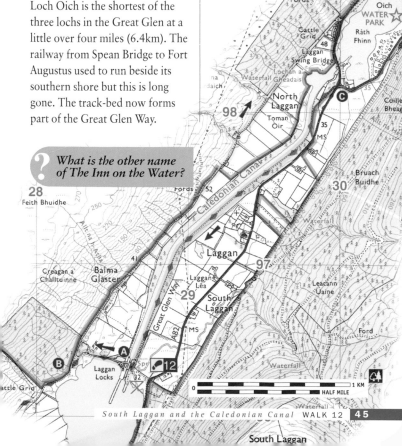

When Telford built the canal this was a double leaf cast-iron bridge. In 1932, when the road along the Great Glen was being improved, this was replaced by the present bridge.

Cross the canal and continue along the A82 to the main entrance to the Great Glen Water Park. Among the many features and attractions that this park has to offer are day trips and boat hire, providing the casual visitor with the chance to get on the canal.

C Cross the road then turn right onto a narrow, gravel-surfaced footpath that heads towards the canal. You are now on the Great Glen Way, Scotland's newest long-distance footpath. Officially opened by Prince Andrew, Earl of Inverness, in April 2002, it follows the line of the Great Glen from Fort William to Inverness a distance of 73 miles (117km).

Continue along the path which joins Laggan Avenue, a magnificent wooded walk along the side of the canal and lined with a wide variety of trees established by Thomas Telford when the canal was originally constructed. Cross a small bridge near the youth hostel and continue to Laggan Locks. Just before the locks, pass a boat known as The Inn on the Water. This is as good a refreshment stop as any when it is open. Continue to the locks then turn left and head back to the car park. ●

Loch Lochy from Laggan Locks

Fort William to Inverlochy Castle

13

START Tourist information centre just off the car park NN103739

DISTANCE 4 miles (6.4km)

TIME 2½ hours

PARKING Fort William town centre (charge)

ROUTE FEATURES Pedestrian precinct; pavements; well-surfaced footpaths; very short section over rough grass and a little boggy ground

Political intrigue, bloody battles and an ancient stronghold combine with the scenery of the prettiest town in the Highlands to make one of the most interesting walks in this book. Combine this with a visit to the West Highland Museum to find out more about the history of the place and to see the famous secret portrait of Bonnie Prince Charlie.

From the car park follow signs towards the tourist information centre. Exit the car park and walk along the side of the information centre, pass the West of Scotland Museum then turn right out of Cameron Square and walk along the pedestrianised shopping street. Continue to the very end of the street then go down some steps, through a pedestrian underpass and up more steps at the other side to reach the rail and bus stations.

A Turn left following the sign for the Old Fort and head across the Safeway car park. Exit onto the pavement beside a Great Glen Way signpost.

The Old Fort is immediately across the road from here.

B Turn right and walk to the end of the roundabout. Cross the road here then turn left and follow the pavement to the left of McDonald's.

PUBLIC TRANSPORT Not needed

PUBLIC TOILETS By the tourist information centre

REFRESHMENTS Loch Hall on the right just past McDonald's at the start of the walk serves food and refreshments. The Café Chardon beside the car park is first class

CHILDREN'S PLAY AREA Available at Loch Hall

ORDNANCE SURVEY MAPS Explorer 392 (Ben Nevis & Fort William)

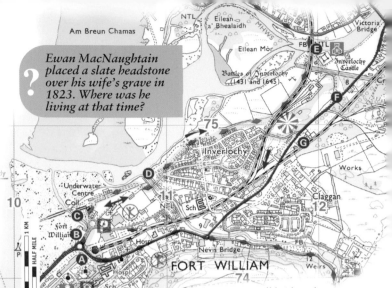

? Ewan MacNaughtain placed a slate headstone over his wife's grave in 1823. Where was he living at that time?

Cross two small bridges then go through a kissing-gate. When the path ends at a lane go through another kissing-gate and turn left. Head along the lane then at the Soldiers Bridge, turn right and go under the railway line.

C Follow the Great Glen Way from here continuing on a tarmac path.

Pass the shinty pitch where on a clear day you can enjoy a splendid view of the mountains at the start of Glen Nevis. Pass through an area of housing following the Great Glen Way signposts.

D Cross a bridge over the river Nevis and, at the far end, turn left onto a footpath. Follow this along the banks of the River Lochy.

E Immediately, cross a stile on your left and follow the faint track across the grass to Inverlochy Castle.

Turn right and go through the large doorway in the castle wall. Explore the interior then exit via a gateway at the other end. Circle the castle from here then leave the grounds through a gate in the wall. Turn right into a lane and follow it until it forks. Keep left at the fork, cross a bridge then continue to the junction with another road.

Cross the road then turn left and walk along the pavement. Follow it to reach a kissing-gate.

F Turn right through this gate and head uphill towards the remains of an old cemetery. As graveyards go, this one is not particularly old but it is neglected and overgrown with several tumbled headstones and very atmospheric.

From the graveyard, cut across an area of marshy ground, along the side of a small industrial complex. Then head up the small hill that rises from the end of the buildings. At the top of the hill you can have a welcome rest on a well-placed bench and look back at the views down Loch Linnhe to the paper mill at Corpach and across the field where the Battle of Iverlochy was fought.

Head back in the direction you've just come then veer right and follow the remains of a hedge. Cross over a stile by the road then turn right and continue along the pavement.

G After about 200 yds (183m) cross a stile on your right and go along a gravel surfaced footpath. This soon changes to a narrow track, which runs behind a hotel.

Keep on the track and eventually cross a footbridge over the railway.

Turn left onto a faint track, which runs to the rear of some houses. This widens to a rough road. Keep on it until it reaches a surfaced road then take the first turning on the right. Turn left at the next junction into Lundy Road. Head along here to another junction beside some shops. Cross the road and continue along the same street, which has now become Wades Road. At the end of this, cross the bridge then follow the Great Glen Way markers back to the station. Return from here to the car park. ●

Inverlochy Castle

14 St John's Church and Loch Leven's Burial Island

START A82 at St John's Church half a mile (805m) west of Ballachulish
Distance 4½ miles (7.2km)
TIME 2 hours
PARKING St John's Church (free)
ROUTE FEATURES Forest roads; forest paths; gentle gradients

This is an easy and attractive walk along forest roads and through tranquil woodlands. It is spectacular in the early evening when the setting sun bathes the land on both sides of the loch with a golden light. The walk offers unrivalled, panoramic views of Glencoe and fascinating glimpses of the ancient and more recent history of the locality.

From the car park in front of the church turn left onto the road and head past the church and the house next to it. Turn left and go through a gate and onto a forest road.

Looking back out over Loch Leven, you'll see the villages of Ballachullish and Glencoe with the distinctive rounded top of Sgorr na Ciche, the Pap of Glencoe, guarding the entrance to the glen. A number of small islands can also be seen. The one just beyond the

Isles of Glencoe Hotel is Eilean Munda, the burial island complete with gravestones and the ruins of a small church, named after St Fintan Mundus, a holy man and relative of St Columba. Fintan himself is supposed to have died in AD 635 but his church remained in use until it burned down in 1495.

Continue along this for just short of a mile and a half (2.4km) to reach a junction. Keep left and continue for a little over half a mile.

PUBLIC TRANSPORT Bus from Fort William
PUBLIC TOILETS Tourist Information Centre Ballachulish
REFRESHMENTS Ballachulish Tourist Information Centre serves food all day including delicious home-made soup
ORDNANCE SURVEY MAPS Explorer 384 (Glen Coe & Glen Etive)

Across the loch from Eilean Munde stood **Callart House**, home of the Camerons of Callart. In the early 17th century an outbreak of the plague infected all of the family except Mary, one of the daughters. The house was ordered to be burnt down with all its inhabitants, but Mary received a warning from her sweetheart. She escaped during darkness and swum naked across the loch where he was waiting with clothes. Fortunately she was free of plague and survived.

Access to the island is to one of three places known as the Ports of the Dead, one allocated to each of the families who used the burial ground. The MacDonalds of Glencoe, Stewarts of Ballachullish and Camerons of Callart all have burial rights. One of the most famous graves on the island is that of MacIain, Chief of the MacDonalds who was slain in the Massacre of Glencoe.

If it's a decent day you should have some great views along the length of Loch Leven, over the Ballachullish bridge to Onich, North Ballachullish, Bishop's Bay and perhaps as far as Loch Linnhe and beyond to the Morven mountains. Looking south from here you should see the two peaks of Beinn a' Bheithir.

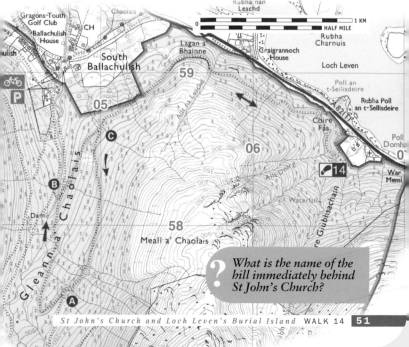

> ? What is the name of the hill immediately behind St John's Church?

In **Ballachulish** a massive, disused slate quarry is all that remains of a once prolific industry. Quarrying had started in 1693 but by the end of the 18th century the new industrial centres of the Industrial Revolution had increased the demand for slate. At their peak the local quarries were producing 26 million slates a year. A decrease in demand coupled with cheaper imports signalled the end of the industry by the mid-20th century.

Of the many interesting gravestones that can be seen, some of the oldest are Celtic graves dating back to the 15th century. They are distinguished by the intricate Celtic designs carved into the entire stone. Like most ancient burial grounds Eilean Munda has a wealth of folklore and tales of the supernatural. In common with other old burial isles, tradition has it here that the last person buried has to remain earthbound and keep watch over the island until relieved by the next departed soul.

There is a bend in the road and just after this is a waymark and the road forks.

A Go right here and head downhill on a lesser used forest road. This will eventually narrow to a very pretty footpath through the woods. Continue downhill into Gleann a' Chaolais for about half a mile (805m) to reach a junction beside a bridge.

B Fork right here and head uphill on another forest road. In another third of a mile (536m) you will reach the junction you passed on the way up.

C Turn left and follow the road back downhill to return to the car park. ●

Loch Leven and the Pap of Glencoe

Ariundle Oakwoods

15

An easy walk on paths through woodlands and moor. The highlight of this walk is the site of the village of Torban, where the lines of the ancient runrigs can still be clearly seen. Although marked as suitable for wheelchairs, there are some boggy and stony parts, which could be difficult for a wheelchair user to negotiate.

START Car park at the Cosy Knits Tea Room
DISTANCE 3 miles (4.8km)
TIME 1½ hours
PARKING One mile north of Strontian on an unlisted road (free)
ROUTE FEATURES Forest roads; well-surfaced footpaths

From the car park turn right onto a forest road and continue past a second car park to reach a waymark pole by a junction.

A Turn right and continue along a narrow footpath. Cross the wooden bridge across the river and turn left onto a path that follows the course of the river.

D To your right was the settlement of Torban, Clan Cameron land first mentioned in records in 1698. Ariundle means the Shieling of the White Meadow and this is where the villagers grazed their cattle in the summer.

The people lived in rough creel houses made from turf or in black houses. Life here would have been very hard. Poor soil and a harsh climate made for a very hand-to-mouth existence. The cattle were assembled in late summer and walked by drovers to the great cattle tryst, or market, at Falkirk. In the depth of winter those few beasts remaining would be bled and their blood mixed with oatmeal to supplement the diet.

Look out for the remains of houses and the ruined walls of enclosures. Crops were grown in narrow strips called runrigs and you can still

PUBLIC TRANSPORT None
PUBLIC TOILETS At car park
REFRESHMENTS Cosy Knits Tea Room at car park
ORDNANCE SURVEY MAPS Explorer 391 (Ardgour & Strontian)

make out their outlines on the land and feel them underfoot in the undulations of the path. The village was abandoned in the early 19th century and the land given over to sheep grazing. The sheep, too, are long gone and soon the hillside will again be covered with trees. More than a million spruce, larch and pine have been planted.

The village of **Strontian** dates from the early 18th century when it was established to provide housing for miners working the local lead mines. At their peak the mines employed some 600 people. Various slumps in the market resulted in the mines closing to reopen again when conditions improved. In 1790, when Britain was at war with France, the mines were providing lead shot for the British Army. The mines closed permanently in 1930.

? *What species of bat might you be able to see in the woods in the evening?*

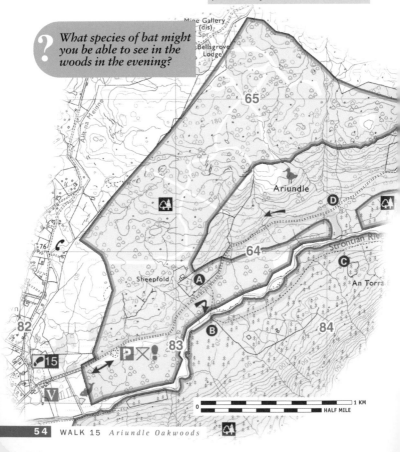

Strontian River near Ariundle

Follow the path from here along the bank of the River Strontian until you reach another bridge.

C Cross this and go through a kissing-gate in the deer fence to enter Ariundle Oakwood National Nature Reserve.

Oak woodlands once covered vast areas of Britain but most disappeared due to clearing for agriculture or burning as fuel. This one survived because it was managed as a coppice woodland. The trees were cut down to stumps from which grew many new shoots. Every 20 years or so the poles would be harvested and the process started all over again.

Farther along this glen are some lead mines. A steady supply of wood was required to convert to charcoal for use in the lead smelters. As the local woodland was felled new trees were planted to replace them. Today, native oak regeneration is being encouraged while the introduced species are being allowed to die off. Native hazel, rowan and birch also flourish within the reserve.

Walk through the woods on specially-constructed duckboards. Look out for the small, tar-like droppings that will tell you that the shy pine-marten has been hunting along here.

The woods are rich in animal and plant life. Spiders, beetles and other insects at the bottom of the food chain feed on the remains of dead and fallen trees. They then become lunch for a host of small mammals like shrews, voles and mice who in turn have to keep a watchful eye for the tawny owl and pine-marten. Buzzards are fond of the smaller birds that flit through the trees – robins, chaffinches and blue tits.

Part of the scrub has been cleared away from the river in the reserve and this is encouraging butterflies. The rare chequered skipper breeds here in the spring but you may also spot the small pearl bordered fritillary, the green veined white, the green hairstreak and Scotch argus, depending on when you visit. Plant life worth looking out for includes bluebells, wood anemones and molinia grass.

D Exit the reserve and turn left onto the forest road. Other birds you may be lucky to see on the way back are redstarts and warblers, tree pipits, spotted flycatchers and even dippers. And if you are particularly quiet there is also the possibility of encountering a roe deer, a fox or perhaps an otter.

Strontian's main claim to fame is its association with a new mineral, **strontianite**, which was discovered in the lead mines there in 1790. The mineral was recognised by a scientist called Adair Crawford and named after the village. Some time later scientists established that the mineral contained a new chemical element, strontium. But it was not until 1808 that Sir Humphry Davy, inventor of the **miner's safety lamp**, isolated it.

Bridge over River Strontian

Castle Tioram

An interesting and varied walk along the rugged shoreline of Loch Moidart, through some woodland and rhododendrons to a narrow cliff path which leads to another beach. Then a short hill climb leads to the forlorn and forgotten remnants of a once bustling community before heading back downhill to the start by way of a picturesque lochan and a reservoir.

START End of the unlisted road which is on the left immediately after crossing Shiel bridge past Acharacle on the A861

DISTANCE 4 miles (6.5km)

TIME 2 hours

PARKING Castle Tioram (free)

ROUTE FEATURES Narrow, muddy and rocky cliff path; heather moorland and bog

Walk along the road by the beach heading in the direction of the castle. Pass a rusting metal gate and continue along the beach to reach the tidal strip that joins the castle with the mainland.

Ⓐ Turn left onto this and visit the castle island.

Castle Tioram makes an appearance in the film *Rob Roy* as the exterior of the Duke of Argyll's castle. It also briefly appears as a scenic shot in *Highlander* and *Highlander 3*.

Built in the 14th century, it was the stronghold of the Macdonalds of Clanranald. During the first Jacobite rebellion of 1715 it was set on fire to make it unavailable for Government use. The chief was subsequently killed at the Battle of Sheriffmuir and the castle has been unoccupied since.

You can only get on the castle island at low tide. *Make sure you return before the tide changes or you'll be stuck there till the next low tide.*

? *What is the name of the island beyond the one the castle sits on?*

PUBLIC TRANSPORT None
PUBLIC TOILETS None on walk
REFRESHMENTS Acharacle
ORDNANCE SURVEY MAPS Explorer 390 (Ardnamurchan)

When you have visited the castle, return to the beach and continue along it. When the beach ends a path continues into woodland. This continues onto the cliff path. Go through a gate and follow the path *taking great care as some of the sections are narrow, muddy and rocky*. Eventually the path will come round a headland to a beach.

About a mile (1.6km) into the walk the path splits at a cairn.

B Turn right and head uphill eventually to reach the abandoned settlement of Briaigh. To see the abandoned township of Port a' Bhata, follow the path straight ahead from the cairn for just under a mile and then retrace your footsteps to the cairn.

> According to the census **Port a' Bhata** had a population of 57 people in 1841 in nine separate households. Ten years later this had declined to 22. The failure of the potato crop in 1846, although not as severe in effect as the one in Ireland, still caused considerable hardship and many people emigrated. At the next census the township had virtually ceased to exist with just one farm remaining and a gamekeeper's cottage.

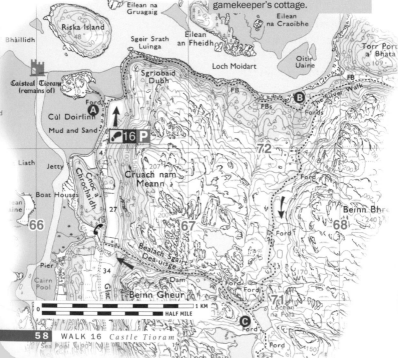

Castle Tioram

There are many abandoned townships in the hills of Moidart. Port a' Bhata (the bay of the boat) is probably the finest example. The people of the townships eked out a subsistence living by cultivating basic crops like bere and barley, in narrow strips called runrigs. Cattle were important as were illicit whisky stills. The notorious Highland Clearances, the failure of the potato crop and a general desire on the part of some people to improve their lives were among the many factors that led to the end of these small communities. All that now remains of Briaigh are the tumbledown ruins of a few cottages.

Keep straight ahead, and uphill, through the township and although the track gets faint for a while it will soon become more established.

Once you have come over the top of the hill you will see below and in front of you a lochan. To the right-hand side are some pine trees. Head downhill following the path towards the right-hand side of the trees.

When the path reaches a solitary hawthorn tree it splits.

C Go right here and follow the path along a gully. Continue towards a reservoir and along the right-hand side of it. At the head of the reservoir the path continues downhill along a glen. At the foot of this go through a gate and follow the line of the fence down to the road. Go across a stile near a red telephone box and turn right onto the road. Follow this to return to the car park. ●

17 *Mallaig*

This walk, though never far from the fishing port of Mallaig, has an atmosphere of remoteness about it. Once over the hill from Mallaigvaig it's not difficult to imagine that you are instead on remote Knoydart just across the loch from here or with Bonnie Prince Charlie on his flight through the heather.

START	Railway station
DISTANCE	5 miles (8km)
TIME	3 hours
PARKING	Mallaig parking bays (charge)
ROUTE FEATURES	Pavement; road; footpaths; boggy open hillside

At the start of the 20th century Mallaig was nothing more than a collection of huts. The way of life of the inhabitants had not changed for centuries. In 1901 the coming of the railway to this remote corner of Scotland brought with it rapid change. The construction of the pier and harbour established Mallaig as one of the principal herring fisheries in Scotland. Nowadays, with the herring all but gone, the fishing fleet concentrates on prawns. Mallaig may no longer be the busy, bustling port it once was but it is still the railhead of the West Highland line, the end of the famous Road to the Isles and one of the finest places to eat seafood in Britain.

From the station, head east through Mallaig. Pass the tourist information centre and then on the left-hand side the East Bay car park. Cross the road and take a path heading up between Tigh Na Craig and the Springbank Guest House. This is marked 'circular walk'. Go through a kissing-gate and follow the well-defined path uphill and then turn left at a large boulder. Nearby are two benches with a grand view back across the harbour.

> **?** *What is the name of the loch behind and to the right of Loch an Nostarie?*

PUBLIC TRANSPORT Train from Fort William

REFRESHMENTS Any of the many restaurants in Mallaig

PUBLIC TOILETS At station

ORDNANCE SURVEY MAPS Explorer 398 (Loch Morar & Mallaig)

From Mallaig there is a small ferry across Loch Nevis to the village of **Inverie** on the Knoydart peninsula. This is the only way into this vast area, known as the 'rough bounds' for there are no roads. It's at least a two-day walk over very rough country to the nearest one. Its highest mountain, Ladhar Beinn at 3343 ft (1021m) is the most westerly Munro on mainland Scotland. It's a popular destination for the hardier types of walker.

When the path forks **A** keep right and follow the lower path. This runs beside a burn for a short distance then crosses it and heads uphill. Near the top **B** there's a signpost. Turn left here and walk a short distance uphill for the views of Skye and the Cuillins and, to the left, the islands of Eigg and Rum. Retrace your path to the signpost and cross the path heading towards Loch an Nostarie. Go through a gate then turn left and follow the waymarked path round the contours of the hill. Just before the second waymark keep a look-out for some interesting quartz rocks.

Past the second post the path curves right and crosses some rough, boggy ground. To the left and below is the hamlet of Malaigvaig. Bonnie Prince Charlie landed here from Skye on July 5, 1746, and was almost captured. Only by hiding under a plaid in the bottom of the boat was he able to avoid being spotted.

Loch an Nostarie

Boats moored near Mallaig

Several tracks cross this section but whichever one you take you will eventually reach another waymarker. Follow the path down into the glen from here keeping to the right of some newly planted woodland. When you have passed another two waymarkers you will be able to see the loch ahead.

C Go through a kissing-gate in a deer fence and keep on the path to another fence where you will have to climb a locked gate.

The area enclosed by the deer fences is part of the common grazing for the crofters of Mallaig. This area once had a thriving woodland but this has all but disappeared from overgrazing and neglect. The fencing is part of a scheme to help restore the area to its former glory by planting native woodland and encouraging natural regeneration. This will benefit both crofters and the environment.

Turn left and follow the track over a small burn then veer right and uphill to a large boulder. There's another waymark just beyond the boulder. Continue on the track, which gets a bit faint at this point but follow the left side of a small glen and you will eventually reach the next waymark, which should be visible in the distance. Just beyond this is a signpost. Pass it and when the track intersects a path turn right, heading for Mallaig via Loch an Nostarie.

Rubha

D Cross a burn via stepping stones then, when the path forks, keep left on the well-trodden path following waymarkers. The path will eventually reach the edge of the loch. Cross a fence here via a stile and continue on the well-waymarked track which, although boggy, now has sleepers crossing the worst parts.

Eventually the path goes past a couple of old buildings with rusting tin roofs, a house and through a gate.

E Turn left onto a lane and follow it as it goes under the railway to reach the road. Turn right and follow the road into Mallaig. Turn left at the junction and return to the station.

18 *The Parallel Roads of Glen Roy*

This relatively rough and strenuous hill walk through thick heather moorland could be described as a beach walk. The beaches in question, however, don't look much like beaches and there has been no sand or water near them for thousands of years. They were created during the last ice age, when glaciers ravaged the landscape to form these unique geological features.

START Car park three miles up Glen Roy from Roy Bridge
DISTANCE 5 miles (8km)
TIME 3½ hours
PARKING In Glen Roy (free)
ROUTE FEATURES Rough heather-covered moorland and hillsides; rough, boggy tracks

Glen Roy is one of the most fascinating glens in Scotland. From the car park look north and, along the sides of the hills, you will be able to see what looks like three roads running along the contours of the hills. These are the 'Parallel Roads of Glen Roy', one of the most famous glacial landforms in the United Kingdom.

? *What is the height above sea level of the first parallel road?*

From the edge of the car park a wide, grassy, path runs up the side of Bohuntine Hill. It's a short distance up to the first 'parallel road' but rather steep so take it easy. When you reach the first road cross over and continue following the path uphill to reach the second. From the car park the roads look as if they will be reasonably wide and provide easy walking. Think this and you are about to experience disappointment.

A Turn right and follow a faint track round the contours of the

PUBLIC TRANSPORT None
PUBLIC TOILETS None
REFRESHMENTS Stron Lossit Inn, Roybridge, serves bar meals, teas and coffees all day
ORDNANCE SURVEY MAPS Explorer 400 (Loch Lochy & Glen Roy)

hill. The ground is rough and covered in thick heather and bracken. The track all but disappears at points and parts of the hillside are steep. *The main thing to remember is to stick to following the contours and eventually you will pick up the track when it reappears.*

According to Gaelic myth, the three roads you see on the hillside were created by the legendary warrior, Fingal, to make it easier for him to hunt.

As you approach the north side of the hill you will have a superb view along Glen Roy with the parallel roads stretching along the hillsides on both sides of the glen. Below you, the single-track road up the glen runs like a slender ribbon alongside the River Roy.

B Circle round the north end of the hill and continue following the tracks along the Lairig Caol. Running along the bottom of this hill pass is the water of Allt coire Ionndrainn. There are a few small burns running down the hillside to this, which you will have to negotiate. They can simply be stepped over.

Again the track will disappear at points but keep heading towards a single, large rowan tree which you should be able to see on the horizon.

Glen Roy, the Parallel Roads

Along the Parallel Roads

in Glen Roy. The whole of the glen was then a huge loch and, as the ice advanced then retreated, the water level of the loch rose then fell. There were three such changes in level and the parallel roads are the shorelines, which were formed at each level. The effect is similar to the tide marks that are left on a bath when the water is drained away.

For centuries, in the absence of any other coherent explanation for the creation of the roads, the belief that they were built by a legendary superhuman was as good an explanation as any. Later, scientific research was to prove that the roads were, in fact, the product of natural forces.

From the tree keep heading in the same direction following tracks as much as possible. Eventually you will reach a conifer plantation.

C Turn left and follow the line of the trees uphill. Cross a gate near the top and keep following the edge of the plantation.

Ten thousand years or so ago, at the end of the last ice age, a massive glacier in Glen Spean provided an effective dam which held the water from the melting ice

Cross two small burns in rapid succession and climb uphill to reach a fence. There are faint tracks running parallel to the fence but the ground here is pretty boggy. Keeping close to the fence is the best line to take.

D Turn left and follow the line of the fence, across the moorland of Meall Dubh, to reach another conifer plantation.

E Turn left here and continue along the fence to reach the end of the trees.

Keep going in this direction and pick up a track on the parallel road.

F Follow this to a solitary tree that sits beside the top of the grassy path, turn right and head downhill back to the car park.

Some of Glen Roy now forms part of a National Nature Reserve managed by Scottish Natural Heritage to ensure the preservation of these important landscape features. ●

Following a daring raid, at Christmas 1645, on the Inveraray headquarters of the Covenanting Clan Campbell, the Marquess of Montrose marched his Royalist forces back to **Fort Augustus**. Receiving intelligence that the Duke of Argyll was behind him at Inverlochy he turned and with 3000 men marched across the snow-filled passes at the head of Glen Roy to arrive above **Inverlochy Castle**. Descending on them at first light Montrose's troops defeated their enemy (see Walk 13).

19 # *Allt Na Caillich Waterfall and the River Garry*

This very magical walk is composed of sections from the five waymarked forest walks at Allt na Cailliche. Walk through a fragment of the ancient Caledonian pine forest, enjoy magnificent views of Ben Tee and the River Garry and take the opportunity to see a wide variety of forest wildlife.

START Forest Gate car park

DISTANCE 5¼ miles (8.4km)

TIME 3 hours

PARKING Forest Gate car park (free) off the A87 two miles (3.2km) west of Invergarry

ROUTE FEATURES Riverside and woodland footpaths; forest and estate roads; hill climb to the waterfall

Follow the green waymarker from the car park onto a well-surfaced footpath along the banks of the River Garry. The name of the river in Gaelic, Gharaidh, means rough and winding. Walk a few yards along its banks and you'll have no doubt that it is aptly named. The flow of the river is controlled by the dam at the end of Loch Garry. The Garry is a famous fishing river but the private owners exercise a tight control over its use. Access by anglers and for canoeing is by permit obtainable from the Invergarry Hotel. Each year Atlantic salmon return from the sea to their birthplace in the Garry. They struggle and fight their way upstream to spawn. The young salmon, or fry, remain in the river until they have grown into smolts then they, too, leave and head out to sea. Anglers catching salmon on the River Garry are encouraged to release any salmon they catch to conserve and increase the stock of fish on the river. Look out for various water birds as you walk along. You may see a solitary heron gliding along looking for a favourite fishing spot or a dipper foraging in the water or bobbing on a rock.

PUBLIC TRANSPORT None

PUBLIC TOILETS None

REFRESHMENTS The Invergarry Hotel does bar meals, dinners, teas and coffees

ORDNANCE SURVEY MAPS Explorer 400 (Loch Lochy & Glen Roy)

About half a mile along the riverside **A** turn left at a waymarker, go through a gate and into woodland. Walk along this pleasant forest road for a few hundred yards (270m) then turn right where there is a single green waymarker on the right and a black one on the left. Head uphill on a well-defined trail through a forest carpeted in moss and in the autumn, with thousands of tiny fungi growing from it. Fungi of all sorts are in abundant supply in the forest here. Look for clumps of honey fungus. This rather destructive fungus is responsible for killing a wide range of trees and shrubs. It is usually found in dense clusters on the trunks of living and dead trees as well as on stumps and roots. Although edible it must be very well cooked and is difficult to digest. Unless you are an expert, it is best to avoid sampling any supposedly edible fungi just in case you get it wrong. The bright red caps with white spots of the fly agaric, looking as if they have just materialised from the illustrations in a book of fairy tales, appear good enough to eat. *They are to be avoided at all costs. Traditionally used as a fly killer, they contain hallucinogenic properties and are poisonous although rarely fatal.*

Honey fungus on a dead tree

Leave the forest and turn right at a waymarker **B**. Follow the path until it reaches a forest road then turn left. Continue until you reach another green waymarker indicating a change of direction to the left and **C** follow the track downhill through the woods.

D Exit the woods at the bottom of the hill and turn right onto a forest road and follow the red waymarkers. **E** When you reach a U-bend in the road turn left and into the woods on a mossy lane, which will narrow to a grassy track heading downhill. Go through a gate at the bottom of the hill, cross a road and continue downhill onto more woodland. Turn right, where a waymarker arrow points to the 'Falls'. Turn left over a bridge and follow red, yellow and blue markers to the falls.

There are two falls both with viewpoints. Immediately after the second falls the paths split.

> **What was the nickname of Edward Ellis, the man who bought Glen Garry Estate in 1860?**

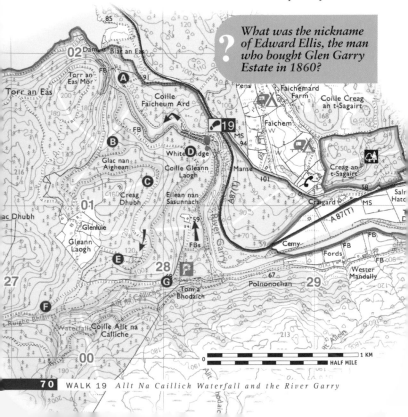

Alt Na Caillich Waterfall

F Turn left and follow the yellow waymarkers uphill. Keep to this path until it reaches a forest road then turn left again. Follow this downhill and through a gate then turn left onto a metalled estate road. **G** Go across a cattle-grid at Forest Gate Cottage, through another gate and turn right onto a forest road.

Pass a car park then take the next road on the right, following yellow and red waymarkers. Go through a turning area and into the wood.

Glen Garry forest contains many areas of Scots pine. This once covered most of the Highlands but the felling of vast areas with little replanting soon denuded and changed the landscape forever. At Glen Garry, Forest Enterprise are managing the Caledonian Forest reserve to protect the ancient woodland and provide the protection it needs to regenerate.

Keep on this well-made path beside the River Garry and eventually the green path will rejoin it. Follow the signs back to the car park. ●

Glen Garry is MacDonell country. Following the battle of Culloden their chief's castle was burned down. A refusal to adopt an English cash economy led to financial ruin and the estate was gradually sold off. Many MacDonell clanspeople were evicted during the Clearances and sought a new life in America. Once Glen Garry was covered in small townships, today all that remains are a few ruins.

Kinlochleven and the story of aluminium

START Car park
DISTANCE 5¼ miles (8.4km)
TIME 3½ hours
PARKING From the B863 in Kinlochleven turn right into Kieran Road. The car park (free) is beside a white church
ROUTE FEATURES Forest paths; rough tracks; land rover tracks; hillside

This walk includes a breathtaking waterfall, spectacular woodlands and some rugged and bleak hillsides. The natural resources and industrial archaeology of the area tell the story of aluminium as the walk progresses through the beauty of the landscape. By its conclusion you will have discovered what transformed a sleepy hamlet to industrial hub and then back again.

Head away from the car park on the footpath that runs along the side of a white church. At a junction turn left. Ignore steps on the right and continue along the footpath. Head uphill then through a gate and keep going to reach a viewpoint overlooking the Grey Mare's Tail waterfall. To the right, a short distance into the woods, is a picnic table.

Continue along the path then head downhill and over a bridge.

In the early years of the 19th century Kinlochleven was a sleepy hamlet of perhaps six houses and a hunting lodge. Because of the surrounding hills and availability of water, it was earmarked to become industrialised. The **North British Aluminium Company** started work on their smelter in 1905 with the construction of a dam, power station and smelter. As a result of the power station, Kinlochleven became one of the first British towns to have electric street lighting.

PUBLIC TRANSPORT Bus from Fort William
PUBLIC TOILETS Just past the Tailrace Inn
REFRESHMENTS Tailrace Inn tea, coffee and snacks all day
PICNIC TABLE On the walk to the falls
ORDNANCE SURVEY MAPS Explorer 384 (Glen Coe & Glen Etive)

A Turn left here and walk along the track a short distance to reach the falls. It is possible to get right up to the pool under the falls but only when the river is low. *However, as the stones and rock are covered in moss and can be very slippery this is not recommended.*

The Grey Mare's Tail waterfall is certainly impressive. Formed by a sheer cliff face at the end of a narrow, wooded gorge, the waters of the Allt Coirena Ba rush over the edge and cascade into a pool 150 ft (46m) below. The falls are best seen after heavy rainfall, particularly in autumn when the narrow ribbon of silver is framed by many shades of gold and brown.

In springtime the fresh green of the trees is enhanced by the masses of bluebells covering the ground.

When you have seen enough of the falls return the same way, passing the bridge and continue along the path by the river. When the path forks keep right following the red waymarker arrows.

B Cross the burn and go uphill on a rough, stony, but well-defined footpath going through two gates and on up through splendid birch woodlands. The path climbs steeply uphill for quite a long way before it levels off. Follow it out of the woods and onto open hillside.

Kinlochleven

The Grey Mare's Tail

Looking back as you climb, the whole of Loch Leven stretches before you and on the sides the rising peaks of Sgurr na Ciche and Beinn na Caillich. Over to your right you will see the six huge pipes, which bring water over the hills from Blackwater reservoir to generate the electricity that was needed to run the aluminium smelter in Kinlochleven. Blackwater was one of the first hydroelectric schemes built in the Highlands, created to provide the huge amounts of electricity needed to run the aluminium smelter. Thousands of Irish navvies (navigators) built the dam to create the reservoir in the years before the First World War. Using only pick and shovel the life of the navvy was

hard. They lived in a hutted encampment by the dam and worked in harsh and unrelenting conditions. Patrick MacGill, one of the navvies, tells the story in his semi-autobiographical novel *Children of the Dead End*. Beyond the pipeline you may see the outline of an old military road that now forms part of the West Highland Way. This was built by General Caufield's troops in 1749-50.

Keep on the path until, in just over a mile (1.6km), it reaches a junction with the track from Mamore Lodge.

This was another property created by the coming of aluminium. Because of a considerable loss of amenity caused by the building of workers' houses in the vicinity of Kinlochleven Lodge, the aluminium company built the estate a new lodge high above the village.

C Turn left and walk along the track for a mile and a quarter (2km) then cross a bridge. Turn left and continue along the road. When you reach a clear area just before some houses **D** turn left and go downhill on a narrow path, cross the river by a bridge and head uphill on a winding path to a junction.

E Turn right and follow blue waymarkers downhill on a rough stony path, crossing several small streams. At the next junction **F** turn left. When you reach the river cross the bridge and head up to the right following the footpath back to the car park.

During the First World War a considerable number of German Prisoners of War were held in a camp at Kinlochleven. During the period 1914-18 they were responsible for building the road, which leads from here along the south side of Loch Leven to Glencoe.

At its peak the **aluminium** smelter employed about 800 people and Kinlochleven was a thriving community with a social club, cinema, school, shops and village hall. After the Second World War mechanisation reduced the numbers of employees. Despite abundant free power and the ability to produce high quality aluminium the facility was not big enough to generate the profits required by a huge multi-national owner and was closed in 2000.

?
Where can you find out all about the history of Kinlochleven's aluminium industry?

Further Information

Walking Safety

Always take with you both warm and waterproof clothing and sufficient food and drink. Wear suitable footwear, i.e. strong walking boots or shoes that give a good grip over stony ground, on slippery slopes and in muddy conditions. Try to obtain a local weather forecast and bear it in mind before you start. Do not be afraid to abandon your proposed route and return to your starting point in the event of a sudden and unexpected deterioration in the weather.

All the walks described in this book will be safe to do, given due care and respect, even during the winter. Indeed, a crisp, fine winter day often provides perfect walking conditions, with firm ground underfoot and a clarity of light unique to that time of the year.

The most difficult hazard likely to be encountered is mud, especially when walking along woodland and field paths, farm tracks and bridleways – the latter in particular can often get churned up by cyclists and horses. In summer, an additional difficulty may be narrow and overgrown paths, particularly along the edges of cultivated fields. Neither should constitute a major problem provided that the appropriate footwear is worn.

Follow the Country Code

- Enjoy the countryside and respect its life and work
- Guard against all risk of fire
- Take your litter home
- Fasten all gates
- Help to keep all water clean
- Keep your dogs under control
- Protect wildlife, plants and trees
- Keep to public paths across farmland
- Take special care on country roads
- Leave livestock, crops and machinery alone
- Make no unnecessary noise
- Use gates and stiles to cross fences, hedges and walls
      (The Countryside Agency)

Useful Organisations

Scottish Natural Heritage
12 Hope Terrace, Edinburgh
EH9 2AS.
Tel. 0131 447 4784
Tel. 0131 446 2277
Email: enquiries@snh.gov.uk
Website: www.snh.gov.uk

Chia-Aig Waterfull

Historic Scotland
Longmore House, Salisbury Place,
Edinburgh EH9 1SH.
Tel. 0131 668 8600
Tel. 0131 668 8669
Website: www.historic
scotland.gov.uk

National Trust for Scotland
Wemyss House, 28 Charlotte
Square, Edinburgh
EH2 4ET.
Telephone 0131 243 9300
Tel. 0131 243 9301
Email: information@nts.org.uk
Website: www.nts.org.uk

Scottish Youth Hostels Association
7 Glebe Crescent, Stirling
FK8 2JA.

Tel. 01786 891 400
Tel. 0 1786 891 333
Email: info@syha.org.uk
Website: www.syha.org.uk

RSPB Scotland
Dunedin House,
25 Ravelston Terrace,
Edinburgh
EH4 3TP.
Tel. 0131 311 6500
Email: rspb.scotland@rspb.org.uk
Website:
www.rspb.org.uk/scotland

**VisitScotland National
Information Centre:**
Email: info@visitscotland.com
Website: www.visitscotland.com
Tel. 0845 2255 121

Public Transport
Website:
www.travelinescotland.com/uk

Fort William Tourist Information Office
Cameron Square, Fort William,
Inverness-shire PH33 6AJ
Tel. 01397 703781
Email: fortwilliam@host.co.uk

Other tourist information centres
Ballachulish: 01855 811296
Fort Augustus: 01320 366367
Mallaig: 01687 462170
Strontian: 01967 402131

Ordnance Survey
Romsey Road, Maybush,
Southampton SO16 4GU.
Tel. 08456 050505 (Lo-call)
Website: www.ordsvy.gov.uk

Ramblers' Association Scotland
Kingfisher House,
Auld Mart Business Park,
Milnathort,
Kinross KY13 9DA
Tel. 01577 861222
Tel. 01577 861333
Email:
enquiries@scotland.ramblers.org.uk
www.ramblers.org.uk/scotland

The River Garry

Loch Leven from the hills above Glencoe Lochan

Ordnance Survey Maps
Explorers
384 (Glen Coe & Glen Etive)
391 (Ardgour & Strontian)
392 (Ben Nevis & Fort William)
398 (Loch Morar & Mallaig)
399 (Loch Arkaig)
400 (Loch Lochy & Glen Roy)

Answers to Questions
Walk 1: August 19, 1745.
Walk 2: Ben Nevis.
Walk 3: 1948.
Walk 4: A sprig of oak.
Walk 5: Nesting boxes.
Walk 6: Corrour Station 13 miles (21km) from the start of the walk. There is no way to reach this station by car.
Walk 7: Dr Alister Sutherland.
Walk 8: It is now the local hospital which is why the lochan is called the Hospital Lochan.
Walk 9: In 1829 at a cost of £697.17.03.
Walk 10: In Loch Linnhe
Walk 11: 1752.

Walk 12: The Eagle.
Walk 13: The Slate Quarrie, Appin.
Walk 14: Meall a' Chaolis.
Walk 15: The pipistrelle.
Walk 16: Riska Island.
Walk 17: Loch an Ghille Ghobaich.

Walk 18: 850 ft (260 m).
Walk 19: The Bear.
Walk 20: The Aluminium Story at Kinlochleven Visitor Centre and Library. (Open April-September, admission free).